MW01503974

Betsy Franco

Illustrated by Ross Watton

DOMINIE PRESS
Pearson Learning Group

ISBN 0-7685-0731-6

Printed in Singapore
2 3 4 5 6   07 06 05

Dominie
Press
Pearson Learning Group

1-800-321-3106
www.pearsonlearning.com

I used to be the only one.

It was just my mom, my dad, and me.

We played games together,

and we read books together.

Now my mom and dad have me
and the triplets!
There are six little socks to put on.
I have fun dressing the triplets.

There are lots of books to read.
I get to read little books to them.

There are so many toys to play with.
The triplets like it when I play
with them.

There are three lunches to fix.
Sometimes I help feed the triplets.

There are thirty dirty fingers to wash.
There are thirty toes to wash, too.
I help with the washing.

At the end of the day,
there are three sleepy little girls.
I help put them to bed.

Then I'm the only one again.
Mom and Dad and I play games
and read my favorite books together.

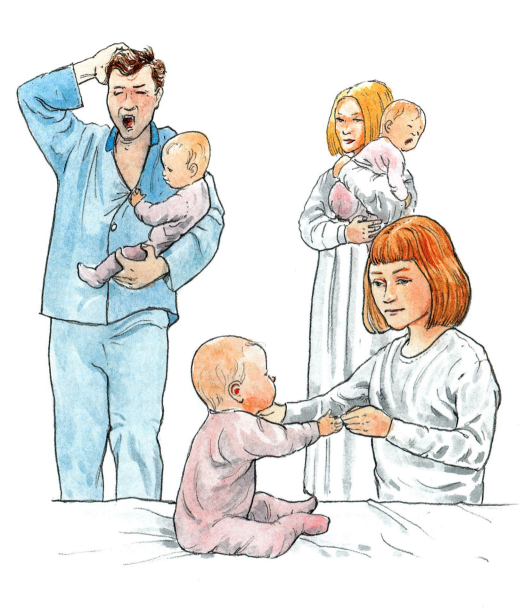

Then in the morning,
it starts all over again.

Now that we have the triplets,
Mom and Dad say
I'm a great big help!